POEMS
POEMAS

Corsino Fortes

POEMS
POEMAS

ENITHARMON PRESS
in association with
poetry translation centre

First published in 2008
by Enitharmon Press
26B Caversham Road
London NW5 2DU

www.enitharmon.co.uk

Distributed in the UK by
Central Books
99 Wallis Road
London E9 5LN

Distributed in the USA and Canada
by Dufour Editions Inc.
PO Box 7, Chester Springs
PA 19425, USA

Poems © Corsino Fortes 2008
Translations from the Portuguese © Daniel Hahn
English versions © Sean O'Brien
Introduction © Daniel Hahn

ISBN: 978-1-904634-76-8

Enitharmon Press gratefully acknowledges the financial support of
Arts Council England, London.

'Letter from Bia d'Ideal' has been published in *Poetry Review*.

British Library Cataloguing-in-Publication Data.
A catalogue record for this book is available
from the British Library.

Designed in Albertina by Libanus Press
and printed in England by
Cambridge University Press

Contents

Introduction	6
Emigrant	9
Letter from Bia d'Ideal	15
The Caesarean of Three Continents	23
When Morning Breaks	27

Introduction

Born and brought up on the Cape Verdean island of São Vicente in 1933, Corsino Fortes undertook his studies in Portugal and spent much of his working life abroad on diplomatic service – notably in Angola and Lisbon.

So while his work is concerned with giving voice to the life of his own country, his perspective is often that of an exile – and the themes of exile and redemptive return recur in his work (see 'Emigrante', p. 9). Having published some of his earlier work in the latter issues of *Claridade* (Clarity), a literary review that defined Cape Verdean literary identity from the later 1930s to 1960 (and gave its name to a prominent movement), Fortes published his first full collection, *Pão & Fonema* (Bread & Phoneme), in 1974. And while much of *Pão & Fonema* was written while Fortes was living outside Cape Verde, like so much of his work, it is concerned specifically with his homeland.

Fortes' use of Cape Verdean Creole – and not just standard Portuguese – in his writing is itself a powerful statement reinforcing the idea of the islands' distinctive African nature. Among the poems from this first collection to be written partly or fully in Creole are 'Carta de Bia d'Ideal' and 'Konde palmanhã manchê' (pp. 15 and 27); in the former, Fortes's friend the poet T. Thio Thiofe (pseudonym of João Varela) is chided for neglecting his Creole to write in Portuguese, the more traditional language of literature – and colonialism.

Pão & Fonema was written and published in the dying days of Portuguese rule in Cape Verde (in the wake of decades of intermittent drought and famine); by the following summer the counter-colonial revolutionary struggle would be won and the archipelago declared independent; the post-colonial dawn of 'Konde palmanhã manchê' had arrived. Yet these are not obviously political poems as we usually understand that term; they do not deal with the country's governments, leaders or freedom-fighting heroes, but present the islands almost mythically – as living places imbued with creative, regenerative forces. Images recur – a pestle, a musical instrument, sun, beach, breasts, bread – physical, inanimate things assigned vital and sometimes epic powers. The poems in this chapbook in particular are significant, in Fortes' words, for the 'telluric and experiential expression' evident in them. By this expression, Fortes seeks to reformulate his re-born country.

The four poems in this volume, and the further six also chosen for translation (selected with the assistance of Stefan Tobler), seek to reflect recurring issues in Fortes' work, as well as a range of style and tone. They are often exclamatory and dramatically musical, offering a particular challenge to the poet tasked with producing an English version, who must seek to recreate this music without sounding, in Sean O'Brien's words, too 'empty and inflated'. It is a challenge made all the more demanding by many of the poems' reliance on recurring images that have no obvious resonance in English; as well, of course, as by the variation between the two languages Fortes employs.

Pão & Fonema was followed in 1986 by *Árvore & Tambor* (Tree and Drum), then in 2001 by *Pedras de Sol & Substância* (Stones of Sun and Substance) – Fortes' only three published collections to date. In 'A Cesariana dos três Continentes' (p. 23), from the opening to the latter collection, he returns to the very birth of the archipelago – not its twentieth-century political rebirth, but its first, prehistoric formation, ten 'navels of stone' set in the sea between the continents of Africa, Europe and America; even the islands themselves are fully animate here, and they heave with creative power.

DANIEL HAHN

EMIGRANTE

Todas as tardes o poente dobra
    o teu polegar sobre a ilha
E do poente ao polegar
    cresce
      um progresso de pedra morta
Que a Península
      Ainda bebe
Pela taça da colónia
Todo o sangue do teu corpo peregrino

Mas quando a tua voz
    for onda no violão da praia
E a terra do rosto E o rosto da terra
    Estender-te a palma da mão
Da oral marítima da ilha
      De pão & pão feita
Ajunturás a última fome
    à tua fome primeira

Do alto virão
Rostos-e-proas-da-não-viagem
    Assim erva assim mercúrio
Arrancar-te as cruzes do corpo

O grito das mães leva-te
    agora
À sétima esquina
    onde a ilha naufraga
    onde a ilha festaja
A sua dor de filha
E a tua dor de parturiente

Que toda a partida É potência na morte
    todo o regresso É infância que soletra

EMIGRANT

Every evening, sunset crooks
    its thumb across the island
And from the sunset to the thumb
    there grows
    a path of dead stone
And this peninsula
    Still drinks
All the blood of your wandering body
From a tenant farmer's cup

But when your voice
    becomes a chord on the shore's guitar
And the earth of the face and the face of the earth
    Extend the palm of the hand
From the seaward edge of the island
    A palm made of bread
You will merge your final hunger
    with your first

From above there will come
The faces and prows of not-voyage
    So that herbal and mercury
Extract the crosses from your body

The screaming of mothers carries you
        now
To the seventh corner
    where the island is shipwrecked
    where the island celebrates
Your daughter pain
The pain of a woman in childbirth

So that all parting is power in death
    all return a child's learning to spell

Já não esperamos o metabolismo
        Polme de boa fruta fruta de boa polpa
A terra
    aspira
        teu falo verde

E antes que teu pé
        seja
            árvore na colina

E tua mão
    cante
        lua nova em meu ventre

Vai E planta
    na boca d'Amílcar morto
Este punhado de agrião
E solver golo a golo
    uma fonética de frescura
E com as vírgulas da rua
  com as sílabas de porta em porta
Varrerás antes da noite
Os caminhos que vão
    até às escolas nocturnas
Que toda a partida é alfabeto que nasce
    todo o regresso é nação que soletra

Aguardam-te
    os cães e os leitões
    da casa de Chota
    que no quintal emagrecem de morabeza

Aguardam-te
    os copos E a semântica das tabernas

No longer do we wait for the cycle
        Pulp from good fruit, fruit from good pulp
        The earth
            breathes in
                your green speech

And there before your feet
                should be
                      a tree on a hill

And your hand
        should sing
                a new moon in my heart

Go and plant
        in dead Amilcar's mouth
This fistful of watercress
And spread from goal to goal
        a fresh phonetics
And with the commas of the street
      and syllables from door to door
You will sweep away before the night
The roads that go
        as far as the night-schools
For all departure means a growing alphabet
    for all return is a nation's language

They await you
        the dogs and the piglets
        at Chota's house
        grown thin from the warmth of the welcome

They await you
        the cups and semantics of taverns

Aguardem-te
as alimárias
amordaçadas de aplauso e cana-de-açúcar

Aguardam-te
os rostos que explodem
no sangue das formigas
novos campos de pastorícia

Mas
    quando o teu corpo
          sangue & lenhite de puro cio
Erguer
    Sobre a seara
A tua dor
E o teu orgasmo
    Quem não soube
    Quem não sabe
        Emigrante
Que toda a partida É potência na morte
E todo o regresso É infância que soletra

They await you
>	the beasts
>	choking on applause and sugarcane

They await you
>	faces that explode
>	on the blood of ants
>	new pastorals to cultivate

But
>	when your body
>>		of blood and lignite, on heat

Raises
>	Over the harvest

Your pain
And your orgasm
>	Who didn't know
>	Who doesn't know
>>		Emigrant

That all of parting is power in death
And all return is a child learning to spell

CARTA DE BIA D'IDEAL

    19 deste mês
    a barlavento das almas que sabiam

Junzin! até na boca de Soncente
Bô nome agora ê Vário ô T. Thio Thiofe
    E Corsa de David dzê
C'ma bô ê um negro negro greco-latino
    Ma! dvera dvera
As ondas
    já trepam
        os degraus do teu poema
E quebram no violão da ilha
Tectos d'Europa
    sob as nossas cabeças

Junzin! há muito
Que não bebes a água
    Da nossa secura
Dvera dvera
Há one driba d'one
    ma cinq'one e um dia

Que pedra ê regode pa sponja dnos coraçon
C'ma spiga de sangue na dor dum concha de lête
Oh dor de cara contente
    dor calode
    dor sentode
    dor lançode —
        ma dor!

LETTER FROM BIA D'IDEAL

  The 19th of the month
  to windward of the souls that knew me

Junzin! Even to the people San Vicente
Your name is Vario or T. Thio Thiofe
   And I, Corsa de David, say
You've become a black black Greco-Latin man
    But really – really
The waves
  already climb
    the steps of your poem
And inside the guitar of the island
The roofs of Europe
    break over our heads

Junzin! A long time now
Since you drank the waters
   Of our thirst
It's true – it's true
Years upon years
   plus five years more, then a day

That the sponge of our hearts has wet the rock
And a conch of milk holds a thread of blood
Oh the pain of a cheerful man!
   silent pain
   pain in repose
   pain cast out
     but pain always

C'ma dor de som na viola
C'ma dor de s'mente na tchon
C'ma dor de vulcon na coraçon —
                      ma hoje!

'M ca ta dzê
      merci
         thank you
            danke schön
               Paquê!

Konde Djosa
    saí porta fora
        c'se caxa d'engraxâ

Tanha morrê na bandera de porta
C'se fome de maçã travessode na boca

Oh pove de Rua de Craca
Alimentode
    nesse colde d'pêxe de 16 toston
Boçes bem ovi
    viola de Patada
        ma
           violão d'Antonzin
Ta rasgâ na sangue de Tanha
    Um silêncio de tantas portas
Boçes bem oiâ
    mostre de navi
        ma
          vela de navi

The ache of the viola's note
Ache of the seed in the earth
Ache of the volcanic heart
           but today

I will not say
    merci
    thank you
        danke schön
            Why?

When Djosa
    went out of the door
        with his shoeshine box

Tanha died by the flag at the gate
With the apple hunger stuck in her mouth

Oh people of the Rua de Craca
Fed
    on fish-broth for 16 tostãos
You all gather to hear
    Patrada's viola
        and
            Antonzin's guitar
Open in the blood of Tanha
    A silence made of many doors
You gather to see
    the ship's mast
    and
    the ship's canvas

Rasgode
quebrode
na oi de Tanha
Paquê! Konde Djosa
Abri na morada
camim de sol aberte

Tanha plantâ na vente
Se boca de maçã mordide

Junzin! 'm tem três cosa
marrode n'alma
Três rios para nunca mais
um scrite na mon
dôs scrite na boca
três scrite na sangue
ê sol ta quebrâ na rotcha
se fome de gema d'ove
ê vente ta mordê na pedra
se grite de farinha bronque
ê pove ma dede de pove
ta screvê na tchon sentença de mon compride
E long time ago
Notcha
já dizia
Ao contrário de Saint-John Perse
Que nem sempre
"O remo rebenta na mão do remador"

Torn
> breaking
>> in Tanha's eyes
>>> Why! When Djosa
Opened in the city
> the sun's open road

Tanha sowed the wind
> with the bitten apple in her mouth

Junzin! Three things
> are bound to my soul
Three rivers for nevermore
> first written on the hand
> then written in the mouth
> then in the blood
on the rock the sun breaks
> the egg of hunger
the wind grinds the stone
> with the flour's white cry
the people and the people's hand
> write the longhand sentence in the earth
And a long time ago
> Notcha
>> was already saying
Saint-John Perse notwithstanding
> That it is not always true
"That the oar will break in the oarsman's hand"

Mantenha da Bibia
Bena
Garda
Vavaia
E tod'esse pove de Rua de Crava

Everybody

Greetings from Bibia
           Bena
           Garda
           Vavaia
And all the people of the Rua da Crava

           Everybody

A CESARIANA DOS TRÊS CONTINENTES

Antes
  da moeda do corpo Ao capital da alma
Antes da luz
  no mar da memória
E da pedra & vento na erosão do rosto
Éramos no verão da terra
  A semente sem primavera
Éramos a exclamação
  Do lon na lunjura
Dando
  Pernas aos montes E braços às montanhas
Dando face & sentido
  Às dunas do mar alto
Que respiram
  as coxas
  os seios
  o sexo de Sahel

Lembro-me de ti! na África do teu ventre
Interrogando-se
  sobre o istmo + a
  proa do nosso destino
Quando pólos e penínsulas de maremoto
Rasgaram & rasgavam
No vórtice da vida! na fractura da terra
  A cesariana dos três continentes

THE CAESAREAN OF THREE CONTINENTS

Before
      the body was coin and the soul *Kapital*
Before the light
      on the remembered sea
And the erosion of the face by stone and wind
We lived inside the summer of the earth
          The seed that had no spring
We were the exclamation
             Of the 'di' in distance
We gave
      Legs to the hills and arms to the mountains
Gave a face and a meaning
      To the dunes of the high seas
That breathe out
        the thighs
        the breasts
        the sex of the Sahel

I remember you! In Africa your womb
Enquiring of yourself
          about the isthmus + the
          prow of our destiny
When poles, peninsulas and tidal waves
Tore and tore
In the vortex of life! In the fracture of earth
          The Caesarean of the three continents

Ficamos umbigos de pedra
                Em rodopio
Entre a pele e o osso das estaçoes
Ficámos então ilha + ilha
                sobre o vento
                    pelo arquipélago da evasão

Assim! foi a pronúncia
                Antes & depois do 1.º dia + a
Erosão da crónica
                na boca da "Rotcha Scribida"

We became navels of stone
                revolving
Between the skin and bone of the seasons
We became island and island
                beyond the wind
                in the evasive archipelago

Thus it was pronounced
                Before & after the 1st day + the
Erosion of the chronicle
                in the mouth of the Written Stone

KONDE PALMANHÃ MANCHÊ

Ó Konde
Ó Konde palmanhã manchê
Konde note ftcha ftchode
E palmanhã manchê
C'pê plantode na tchon
E terra na coraçon
Konde sangue rasgâ na corpe
Arve de broçe aberte
E smente gritâ na rotcha
Tambor de boca verde
E daquel som
Ma quell sangue soldode
Nascê boca
    boca centrode
    boca rasgode
Na roda de sol

Ó Konde palmanhã manchê
Sem dsuspère pundrode
Na bandêra de porta
Sem lanterna cindide
Na robe de burre
Pa naufroge de navi
Sem navi quebrode
Na boca de pove
E mar bem olte! brobe!
    dsusperode
Ben quebrâ na Praia Grande
Sês broçe gorde de pecode
E mar bem
Na se luxe
E na se grandèza!
    Se mostre

WHEN MORNING BREAKS

Oh when
Oh when the morning breaks
And the night becomes more night
When the morning breaks
With its feet on the ground
And the earth in its heart
When blood flows from the body
Like a tree with open arms
And the seed shouts from the rock
Like a green-mouthed drum
And from that sound
That warrior's blood
Mouths are born
      centred mouths
      torn mouths
In the wheel of the sun

Oh when the morning breaks
Without hanging its despair
On the flag of the door
Without lighting torches
On the donkeys' tails
To bring wrecks
Without shipwrecks
On the people's tongues
Then the desperate sea – very high –
      Bravo!
Will come to break on Praia Grande
On its fat sinful arms
And the sea will come
In its luxury
In its grandeur
Showing its mast

De mar erguide na pêto
Se mapa bronque
Desenhode n'alma
Bem bidê na colónia dnha boca
Tod'aquel negoce dnha sangue ultramarine

Ó Konde palmanhã manchê
E Criste bem dsê morada
El bem ta bem
Pa broçe direita de Monte Cara
C'se cobe d'enxada
Ma se calçon drill
C'se pê na tchon
Ma se dede quebrode
Bem sentâ
Na pedra radonde dnôs fogon
Sem tchuva na mon
Sem fraqueza na sangue
E sem corve na coraçon

Ó Konde
Ó Konde palmanhã manchê

On the heart's rough seas
Its white map
Drawn on the soul
Will come to drink in my colonized tongue
All the history of my ultramarine blood

Oh when the morning breaks
And Christ descends from his dwelling
And comes
To the right arm of Monte Cara
With the handle of his hoe
And his drill shorts
Barefoot
With a split finger
And sits down
At our round cooking-stone
With no rain in his hand
No weakness in his blood
No crow in his heart

Oh when
Oh when the morning breaks